IVER JOHNSON HANDGUNS 1871-1941

The Handguns of Johnson & Bye & Co 1871-1883, Iver Johnson & Co 1883-1891, Iver Johnson Arms & Cycle Works 1891-1941

By
Brian L. Massey

© 2015 Brian L. Massey

All Rights Reserved

ISBN 978-0-9940751-1-6

Table of Contents

Iver Johnson 1841-1895 1
Martin Bye 1840-1906 4
Johnson Bye & Co 1871-1883. Iver Johnson & Co 1883-1891. Iver Johnson Arms & Cycle Works 1891-1993. 6
Hero and Uncle Sam: 1871-1873 13
Eclipse and Star Single Shot Cartridge Derringer: 1871-1899 14
Defender: 1873-1888 15
Defender 89: 1889 – 1895 17
Lovell Safety Double Action Model 1879: 1883-1889 18
Gem Blank Pistol: 1880-1890 20
British Bulldog: 1881-1883 21
American Bulldog First Model: 1882-1886 22
American Bulldog Second Model: 1885-1897 24
American Bulldog Third Model: 1898-1899 25
Boston Bulldog: 1887-1899 26
1900 Double Action First Model: 1900-1908 27
Model 1900 Target Small Frame: 1925-1928 30
1900 Target Large Frame: 1921-1941 31
Target Sealed 8 First Model: 1932-1941 32
Lovell Safety Hammer Automatic (Eagle): 1887-1889 34
Lovell Safety Hammerless Automatic: 1887-1889 35
Lovell Swift Hammer: 1890-1894 36
Lovell Swift Hammerless: 1890-1894 37
Safety Automatic Hammer First Model: 1894-1896 38
Safety Automatic Hammer Second Model: 1896-1908 40

Safety Automatic Hammer Third Model: 1909-1941 41
Safety Automatic Hammerless First Model: 1895-1896........42
Safety Automatic Hammerless Second Model: 1897-1908..43
Safety Automatic Hammerless Third Model: 1908-1941.....44
22 Supershot: 1928-1931 45
22 Supershot Sealed Eight: 1931-1941 1945-1957 46
U.S. Revolver Co. Automatic Hammer: 1910-1935 47
U.S. Revolver Co Automatic Hammerless: 1910-1935...........48
Secret Service Special Hammer: 1912-circa 1923 49
Secret Service Special Hammerless: 1912-circa 1923 51
Credits 54

Iver Johnson 1841-1895

Iver Johnson.

Iver Johnson is perhaps the most overlooked firearms designer and manufacturer in America. While Colt and Smith & Wesson are household names, Iver Johnson is almost forgotten. Yet his company produced millions of firearms between its founding in 1871 and its closing in 1993.

Iver Johnson was born on Saint Valentine's Day 1841 in the district of Stryn Nordfjord Norway. He was the son of John Johansen and Berthe Johnsdr. Iver was one of at least three children having an older brother Peter born in 1835 and a younger sister Christie born in 1843. Iver's father John was a farmer and fisherman of little wealth. Life was hard in Nordfjord in the 19th Century. It is a land of high mountains, fjords, glaciers and forests. Since he was not the eldest son it is doubtful he would inherit the family farm. With no future to be found on the farm and little education available in Nordfjord, young Iver left home in 1857 at the age of 16 to be apprenticed as a gunsmith in Bergen. Life was not easy in Bergen working 12 to 16 hours a day but Iver was determined to better himself. In 1862 he finished his training and moved to Oslo to work as a gunsmith. Being a man of ambition and seeing better opportunities in the United States he emigrated from Norway in 1863 setting up shop in Worcester Massachusetts. At the time Worcester was a bustling manufacturing centre producing goods for the Civil War so it was a logical place for Iver to start a business.

1865 Census showing Iver Johnson at age 24.

Iver's business went largely unnoticed for the first few years. He did some gunsmithing for the local market and some design and small scale manufacturing. His most notable work was for Allen & Wheelock. Allen & Wheelock, later known as E. Allen & Company, was a large firearms manufacturer who contracted out some of their production to other small scale operations.

By 1868 Iver was doing well for himself and on April 9th he married Mary Elizabeth Speirs in Worcester, with whom he would later have 3 sons and 2 daughters. Mary was the attractive 20 year old daughter of John and Jennette Speirs. John was a Master Machinist and respected member of the community.

In 1871 Iver formed a new company with Martin Bye which they called Johnson Bye & Company. Martin Bye was another small gunsmith who had also emigrated from Norway in the early 1860s. Iver was not only a skilled gunsmith and designer but he was also a shrewd business man. He purchased Bye's interest in the firm in 1883 and the company name changed to Iver Johnson & Company. The company continued to prosper and Iver became a wealthy man. In 1895 he was worth over $500,000.00 that is about 15 million in 2015 dollars. However his hard-earned wealth could not save him from what Dickens called the "*scourge of mankind.*" Iver Johnson died of Tuberculosis August 3rd 1895 at the age of 54 and was buried in Hope Cemetery in Worcester Massachusetts.

The Grave of Iver Johnson, Hope Cemetery in Worcester Massachusetts.

Martin Bye 1840-1906

Martin Bye was born as Martin Olesen on the 29th of September 1840 in Royken, Buskerud, Norway to Ole Talatsen & Oline Hansdr. At some point in his early life he started using the surname of Bye. He most likely came to America around 1863 but no record of his arrival has been found. He enlisted as Martin Bye in Co. F, 42nd Massachusetts Infantry on 20 July 1864. By May 1865 Martin was no longer in the Army and was living with another Norwegian, Christopher Gunderson and his family in Worcester Massachusetts. It is interesting to note that Christopher was also a gun maker. Martin became an American citizen 21 April 1866 and two years later he married Christopher Gunderson's sister Maria.

1868 Marriage record of Martin Bye and Maria Gunderson.

Martin and Maria had 5 children between 1868 and 1880 - Gilbert, Jennie aka Julia, Alfred Oscar, Emma and Harold Martin. Little Harold the last born, died in January 1880. That same year Martin's wife died of consumption. He needed a wife to look after his young family so he married again in 1881 to the widow Marie Lindstrom nee Thompson. With his second wife Martin had two more sons, Frederick and Warren.

1880 Census showing Martin Bye and family.

Martin started his partnership with Iver Johnson in 1871 but the two men may have known each other before. Being about the same age and both being gunsmiths from Norway it's entirely possible they apprenticed or worked together before coming to America. The partnership was financially successful but only lasted 12 years, with Iver Johnson buying Martin's interest in the company in 1883. The reason the partnership ended is not known. Did the two men have a falling out? Did Iver make Martin an offer he could not refuse? It is known that Martin continued to work in the firearms industry for many years after Iver bought him out so we can guess he was not tired of the firearms industry. Martin died of cancer and nephritis on 29th April 1906 at the age of 65. He was buried in Hope Cemetery not far from his old business partner Iver Johnson.

Johnson Bye & Co 1871-1883. Iver Johnson & Co 1883-1891. Iver Johnson Arms & Cycle Works 1891-1993.

In 1871 Iver Johnson and Martin Bye merged their small gunsmithing operations to form the Johnson Bye & Company. The new company rented a small shop on Church St in Worcester Massachusetts. For several years Iver Johnson had been engaged as a subcontractor by E. Allen & Company in the making of pepperbox revolvers. The new company had intended to continue the manufacture of Pepperbox Revolvers, however they soon began the manufacture of small single shot pistols as well as simple revolvers. Some of the first firearms to emerge from the new firm were a low cost single shot percussion pistol known as the Uncle Sam or Hero, the Eclipse single shot cartridge pistol and the Defender revolver. These simple firearms were much easier to manufacture than the pepperbox revolvers Iver Johnson had made in the past. We can only speculate as to the reason the new company chose to start with such simple designs. It may have been that the simple designs would be quicker to get into production or perhaps the new partners spotted a market that they believed would be profitable. They were also probably well aware that the days of the pepperbox revolver were over. Whatever the reason this decision to start producing simple low cost weapons would prove successful and would set the pattern for the company for the next 120 years.

The new company was doing well focusing on the production of cheap self-defence weapons for the masses. Late 19th century America was a time of violence and people were eager for firearms to protect themselves. American cities were growing at an unprecedented rate and violent crime was an ever-present danger. Westward expansion was continuing and settlers going west wanted firearms.

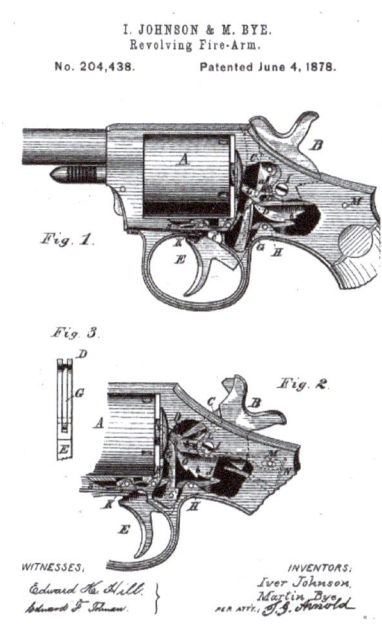

1878 Patent.   *1890s Lovell Arms Co advertisement.*

In 1873 the company was doing so well it had out grown its small room on Church St so they moved to a building on Central St where they took two rooms and employed about 50 men. In 1875 they purchased the building and gradually moved the existing tenants out so that by 1881 they were using the entire building.

In 1881 they signed a contract agreeing that all of their products were to be sold solely by the John. P. Lovell Arms Co. Martin Bye had served with John Lovell's son Benjamin in the 42nd Massachusetts Infantry during the Civil War. In 1876 Iver Johnson named his second son John Lovell. This suggests that the relationship was extremely important and started well before 1881. Established in 1840 J.P. Lovell Arms Co was a large and successful manufacturer, wholesaler, and retailer of firearms and other sporting goods. This important contract with Lovell was maintained when the partnership of Johnson and Bye was dissolved in 1883. Beginning in 1876 Johnson and Bye filed for, and were awarded, several new firearms features and firearms feature improvement patents including an 1878 double action revolver improvement.

Despite the apparent success of the partnership between the two men Iver purchased Martin's interest in the firm in 1883. We don't know the reasons behind the split but the company continued to prosper under the new name of Iver Johnson & Company. It is of note that by this time the company was manufacturing a large variety of goods in addition to firearms. It is beyond the scope of this book to list everything the company made during its 100 plus years but some of the items include air guns, police equipment such as handcuffs and leg irons, bicycles, motorcycles and tools.

In 1891 the company's name changed again to Iver Johnson's Arms & Cycle Works and the company relocated to Fitchburg Massachusetts in order to have better and larger manufacturing facilities. The bicycle industry was booming in the late 19th century and Iver was not going to miss this opportunity. In 1894 production began of the revolver that would become probably the best know Iver Johnson firearm. The Safety Automatic Hammer and its counterpart the Safety Automatic Hammerless would be sold by the millions for almost 50 years.

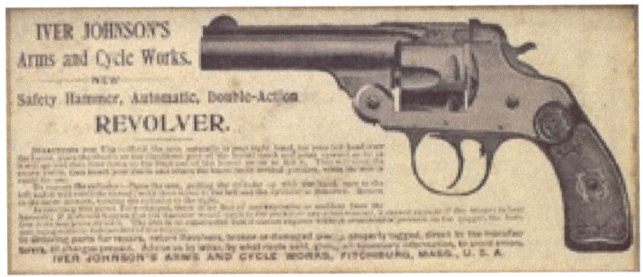

Safety Hammer Automatic.

Fitchburg in the late 19th Century with the Iver Johnson factory center right.

Sales were booming when Iver Johnson died in 1895. The company sold 10,000 bicycles that year and employed about 350 workers. Iver's wife took over as trustee and his young sons took over the running of the business. The company continued to expand. The year after Iver's death, the company issued their first catalog and opened two retail stores.

In 1900, the company made a bold move and acquired the J.P. Lovell Co, which was previously the exclusive retailer of all Iver Johnson products. Lovell Co owned retail stores in New York City and Boston, and also sold to many large mail order houses like Sears & Robuck. In 1901 the company received some perhaps negative publicity when President William McKinley was assassinated with a .32 caliber Iver Johnson Safety Automatic. However the assassination did not affect their sales as far as we know.

Iver Johnson Factory circa 1910. The largest Gun Factory in the U.S.

By 1903 with sales still growing, they opened sales offices in Chicago, New York City, San Francisco, Constantinople, Hamburg Germany, London England and Paris France. However sales outside the U.S. would never reach the quantities the company hoped for.

Motorcycle manufacturing and sales began in 1907. This was probably a logical evolution for the company as they had been a successful bicycle manufacturer for decades. However sales proved disappointing and the endeavor was relatively short lived. In 1909 the company began manufacturing firearms for use with the more powerful smokeless powder cartridges. Smokeless powder had slowly been replacing black powder in firearms ammunition starting in the 1890s. This change required the use of harder steel to withstand the increased pressure. From a manufacturing standpoint it was not a big change and was not noticeable to the casual observer.

Starting around 1910, the company began to a slight shift in their priorities from self-defense weapons to more sporting firearms like shotguns and large frame .22 rim fire target revolvers. However this shift was gradual as they continued to manufacture and sell hundreds of thousands of the Model 1900 and the Safety Automatic each year. It was also in 1910 that a family legal dispute erupted between Iver's widow Mary and their son Fred. Mary had been named as trustee in Iver's will but now 15 years later with the company worth several million dollars, it seemed that Fred felt his Mother was taking more than her fair share as trustee. Despite the legal issues the firearms business continued to grow and over time the company would be restructured to again focus on the firearms business, as they shut down non-firearms concerns such as the motorcycle business in 1916.

A selection of Iver Johnson advertisements from 1911.

World War 1 would give firearms sales another small boost and although Iver Johnson received no Military contracts during the War it was still more profitable to manufacture firearms and tools. War can be good for the firearms trade even without Government support as it contributes to a general feeling of apprehension with in turn fuels civilian sales. These decisions to focus on firearms and tools most likely played a role in the company surviving the Great Depression of the 1930s. During hard times people don't purchase luxury goods like bicycles and motorcycles however they will purchase firearms due the higher rates of armed robbery and crime in general brought on by hard times.

The start of World War 2 in 1939 brought great success to many American companies but Iver Johnson missed out on most of the war time boon. They did sell a small number of handguns to the English who at the start of the war were desperate for anything they could get. But this was a drop in the bucket compared to the millions of firearms produced by other American Companies. The missed opportunities of the War and perhaps the discontinuation of some of the company's most popular firearms signaled the beginning of a slow downward spiral for Iver Johnson. In 1953, Iver's grandson Luther Otto III became president but he was unable to turn the company around. The company continued to concentrate its efforts on low cost sporting firearms. Ironically one of these sporting firearms (an eight shot .22 caliber Cadet 55-A revolver) was used by Sirhan Sirhan to assassinate Robert F. Kennedy on June 5, 1968.

Around 1973 the company was purchased by Louis Imperato. After over 100 years the business founded by Iver Johnson was no longer in family hands. In 1977 Imperato purchased the Plainfield Machine company in Middlesex New Jersey. Plainfield was currently producing M1 carbines from surplus parts. Imperato moved the Iver Johnson factory from its longtime home in Fitchburg to New Jersey in the fall of 1977 and later to Jacksonville Arkansas. The company would continue to operate under the Iver Johnson name until the end finally came in 1993.

Hero and Uncle Sam: 1871-1873

The Hero was perhaps the first firearm manufactured by Johnson & Bye & Company. It was sold under several names including Uncle Sam and Hero. This smoothbore, muzzle loading, percussion single shot pistol was available in .28, .30, or .36 cal. with a 2 1/4 inch barrel. It was manufactured with a one piece frame and barrel, a spur trigger and center mounted hammer. Unlike other Johnson & Bye products from this time that were available in nickel finish the Uncle Sam and Hero were only available in a brown finish. By 1871 the percussion system was technically obsolete. However many customers were skeptical of the new metallic cartridge ammunition preferring the more familiar and lower cost percussion system.

Eclipse and Star Single Shot Cartridge Derringer: 1871-1899

Star with factory engraving and bone grips.

One of the first products offered by Johnson Bye & Company, the Eclipse was a simple single shot break action pistol with a spur trigger. Available in a small frame .22 rimfire with a 2 inch barrel, and a large frame .32, or .38 rimfire with a 2 13/16 inch barrel, the Eclipse was a low cost, close range personal defense weapon. The lack of sights together with a short smoothbore barrel makes a weapon that is only accurate out to a few yards. The low power rimfire cartridges are of limited stopping power, and being a single shot firearm the user would only have one chance to defend himself. The gun was made with a heavy nickel finish that is typical for the time period, and available with wood, hard rubber, or mother-of-pearl grips. A deluxe engraved version called the Star was also offered; it featured an engraved frame and fancy grips. Unlike most break action firearms we see today which are top-break, the Eclipse is a side-break action. To operate the firearm the user swings the barrel to the side to load a single cartridge. The user then swings the barrel closed and raises the hammer to make the weapon ready. Production of this model by Johnson Bye & Company and later by Iver Johnson and Company is believed to number about 15000.

Defender: 1873-1888

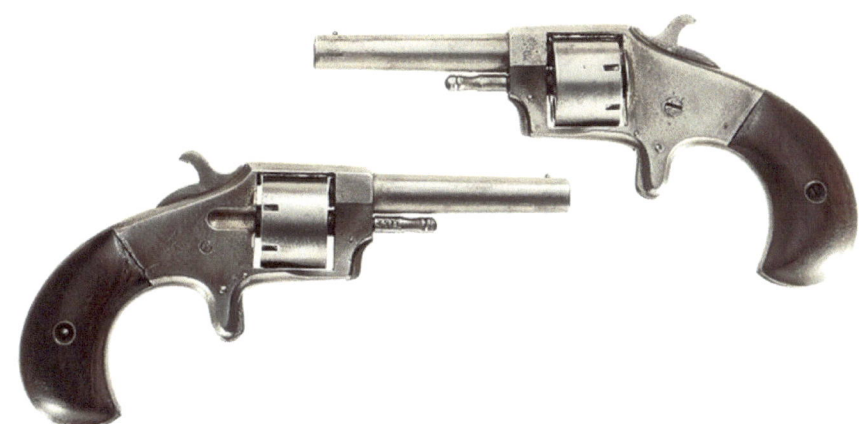

Smoker in .22 rimfire.

Sometimes known as bird's head models after the style of grip the Defender was marketed and sold under many names including Eagle; Encore; Enterprise; Eureka; Favorite; Invincible; J.S.T. Co; J.T. Johnson; Lion; Navy favorite; Old Hickory; Red Hot; Smoker; Tiger and Tycoon. Often these firearms are referred to as brand name revolvers as they were intended to be sold by large mail order companies. The majority of the Defenders and later the Defender 89 were sold by the J.P. Lovell Company of Boston Massachusetts.

The Defender is a solid frame single action revolver with a spur trigger. It was available in a 7 shot small frame .22 rimfire, a medium frame 5 shot .32 rimfire, or a large frame 5 shot .38 or .41 rimfire. All models had a heavy nickel finish and were available with birds head walnut grips.

With prices in 1882 from $1.50 for the .22 rimfire and $5.60 for the .41 rimfire, the Defender was intended as a low cost revolver that everyone could afford. The Defender proved to be a highly successful product for Johnson & Bye and later Iver Johnson. Production started in 1873 and it is believed that over a million Defenders and the Defender 89 were made. Serial numbers went from 1 to 99999 and then restarted again at 1 making it difficult to date the firearms using the serial numbers.

Smoker in .32 Rimfire (top). Eureka in .22 Rimfire (bottom).

Defender 89: 1889 – 1895

In 1889 Johnson & Bye introduced an improved version of the Defender. The Defender 89 was available in the same calibers and was marketed under all the same names as the original Defender. Improvements in the Defender 89 included a fluted cylinder and a choice of round or octagon barrels. However many Defender 89s can be found with the old style non-fluted cylinder. Grips were now available made from wood or hard rubber in the original bird's head style or a new square butt style.

Defender 89 in .32 rimfire.

Lovell Safety Double Action Model 1879: 1883-1889

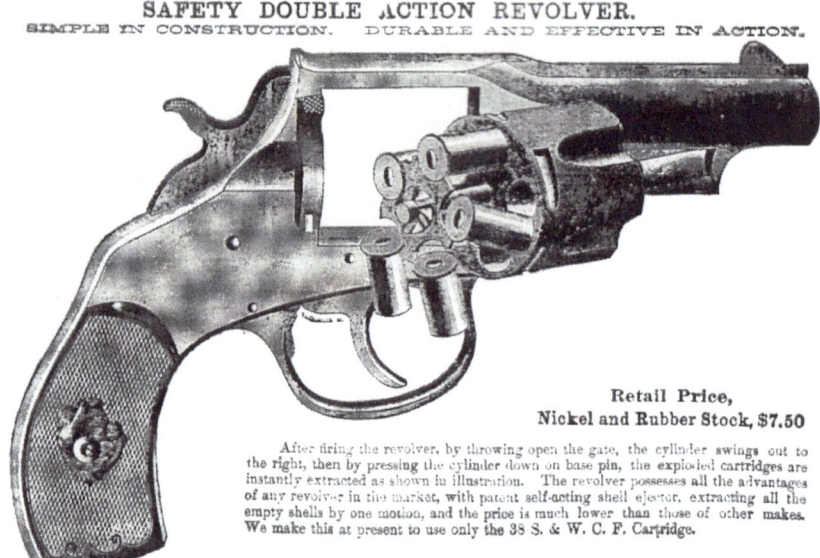

Lovell Model 1879.

The Lovell Model 1879 which only sold through the J.P. Lovell Company of Boston Massachusetts was the first double action revolver with a side swing cylinder manufactured in the United States. To load or unload the revolver the cylinder swings out to the right. This side swing cylinder proved expensive to make and awkward to use and as a result the Model 1879 did not sell well. The Lovell was significantly more complex than previous Iver Johnson revolvers. The Lovell's double action lock and side swing cylinder had more parts and required more sophisticated machining than earlier products like the defender. This complex manufacturing may be the reason for the three year delay between the design in 1879 and production in 1883. Unlike many Iver Johnson firearms that were available in many different variations the Lovell was made only in 38 S&W with a 5 shot cylinder and a 2 7/8 inch barrel. Like many early low cost revolvers the frame and barrel are made from one piece. The Lovell is marked only with "Iver Johnson Co. Maker"

Lovell Model 1879.

The Lovell was available in nickel finish only, with hard rubber dogs head design grip panels. This is one of the rarest Iver Johnson double action revolvers ever manufactured with numbers estimated between 8 and 10 thousand.

Gem Blank Pistol: 1880-1890

The Gem was a .22 rimfire blank firing pistol made in the style of a single shot Derringer. It had a spur trigger and a Flobert type action. While not a real firearm as it was not designed to fire a projectile, improper use could and did result in injuries. It was not uncommon for individuals to attempt to modify the Gem to fire real 22 ammunition. In the late 19th and early 20th Century shooting firearms into the air was a socially acceptable way to celebrate important events. However as one can imagine this custom caused all kinds of safety issues. Blank firing guns were sold as a safer alternative. Blank firing guns were also marketed as an effective means to ward off dogs and other dangers.

British Bulldog: 1881-1883

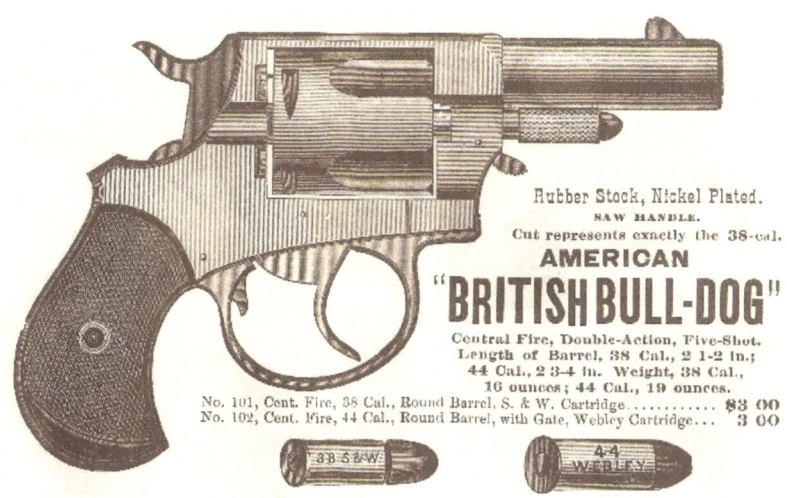

In 1872 P. Webley & Sons of Birmingham England introduced a new revolver known as the British Bulldog. This new revolver became so popular that manufacturers in Belgium, Spain, France and the United States began to copy the design. In 1881 Johnson & Bye & Company introduced a Bulldog style pistol with the words "British Bulldog" stamped onto the top strap. Available in .44 Webley or .38 S&W, the .44 had a hinged loading gate and a 2.75 inch barrel. The .38 had a 2.5 inch barrel and no loading gate. At first glance the Iver Johnson British Bulldog resembles its contemporaries, however it can be identified by the pull pin cylinder and lack of extractor rod. Production was brief from 1881 until the partnership of Johnson & Bye dissolved in 1883. Serial numbers only made it to 5 digits. It was still for sale by merchants in 1884 at a cost of $5.00 but by that time the new firm of Iver Johnson and Company was making an improved version called the American Bulldog.

American Bulldog First Model: 1882-1886

An attempt to improve upon the design of the British Bulldog resulted in the American Bulldog. The new design had an extended rear frame section to improve the user's grip. This new saw-handle grip contour also resulted in a new style of grip plate molded in hard rubber with an American Eagle design of which there were two distinct versions. The American Bulldog was available in four frame sizes and seven calibers, a small frame .22 rimfire, medium frame .32 rimfire & .32 S&W centerfire, large frame .38 rimfire & .38 S&W centerfire, extra-large frame .44 Webley and .44 Bulldog. The barrel length and shape on the small, medium & large frame was 2 ½ inches round or 4 ½ octagon. The extra-large frame was available with a 2 7/16 inch or 4 ½ inch octagon, or 4 ½ inch or 6 inch barrel that was part octagon and part round. The only finish available was nickel plate.

Most first model American Bulldogs have the name stamped on the top strap of the frame however some may be stamped "BRITISH BULL DOG". You can identify first model American Bulldogs as the top portion of the front grip strap is an extension of the rear of the trigger guard. It should be noted that while the Iver Johnson Company may have called this revolver the American Bulldog it was marketed and sold by many different brand names - Ajax Army, Lion, Navy Favorite, Old Hickory and perhaps others.

American Bulldog First Model in .38 Rimfire with a 4 ½ inch barrel.

American Bulldog First Model in .44 Rimfire with a 4 ½ inch barrel.

American Bulldog Second Model: 1885-1897

A second pattern of the American bulldog emerged in 1884 with a slightly modified frame contour which now had a more rounded shape at the rear. Stock plates were finally checkered with the head of a Bulldog or an American Eagle design. The extra-large frame .44 and large frame .38 used the dog's head grips while the medium frame .32 and small frame .22 for the most part still used the eagle grips. Changes were also made to the front grip strap, as it now formed an integral part of the frame rather than being an extension of the rear of the trigger guard. Available calibers and finishes were the same as the first pattern, however the small frame now came with a 2 ¼ barrel. Some late production models of the medium frame .32 had an octagon barrel. Longer barrel lengths were available on medium, large and extra-large frames. This revolver can be identified by the markings: "AMERICAN BULL DOG" on the top of the barrel. Again like the first pattern it was sold and marketed under the names Ajax Army, Lion, Navy Favorite, Old Hickory and perhaps others.

American Bulldog Third Model: 1898-1899

The Third Model American Bulldog was almost identical to the Second Model. However it was now marked Model 1898. This was in all likelihood simply a marketing ploy designed to make customers feel they were getting an up to date design. Some people feel no Third Model exists.

Boston Bulldog: 1887-1899

Boston Bulldog in .32 Smith and Wesson.

The Boston Bulldog was almost identical to the second model of the American Bulldog. However the Boston was only available in three calibers; small frame .22 rimfire, medium frame .32 S&W centerfire, and a large frame .38 S&W centerfire. Made with octagon barrels of 2 1/4 inch length for the small frame or 2 15/32 inch for the large frame, the entire revolver was nickel finish with grips made of hard rubber. The small and medium frame revolvers had grips with a scrolling vine design while the large frame had grips with a dog's head and scrolling vine design. Boston Bulldogs can easily be identified as all are marked on the barrel.

Boston Bulldog in .32 Smith and Wesson.

1900 Double Action First Model: 1900-1908

Introduced in 1900 this revolver in many respects was just a rework of the American Bulldog revolvers. The 1900 was a simple solid frame, double action revolver with a pull pin cylinder release and octagon barrel. The standard finish was nickel plate with a blue trigger guard and hammer. An all blue finish was optional, however they are not seen as often as the nickel plated. Grip panels were hard rubber with an Owl's head logo. The 1900 was offered in three frame sizes and four calibers. Barrel length on the small frame was 2 ¼ inches, and on the medium & large frame it was 2 ½ inches.

Top Strap of a Model 1900 .22 Rimfire.

It should be noted that the large frame model was not introduced until 1903. From 1900 to 1903 the frame used was that of the earlier American Bulldog. Other barrel lengths were offered at an extra charge but not often found. The small frame was offered in .22 rimfire with a 7 round cylinder. The medium frame was available in .32 rimfire and .32 S&W centerfire with 5 round cylinders. The large frame was only available in .38 S&W centerfire with a 5 round cylinder.

Model 1900 Small Frame .22 Rimfire.

1900 Double Action Second Model: 1909-1941

The 1900 Second Model was simply the First Model upgraded to use smokeless powder. The cylinder and internal parts were hardened to take the increased pressure that smokeless powder loads generated. In 1921 a large frame six shot chambered in .32 S&W Long was introduced.

Model 1900 Target Small Frame: 1925-1928

Built on the small frame Model 1900 .22 rimfire, this double action revolver came with a 7 shot pull pin cylinder. It was available with 6 or 9 inch octagon barrels, blue finish overall and oversize two-piece checkered wood grips. The introduction of this revolver was part of the Iver Johnson Company's shift away from self-defense firearms to sporting arms after the First World War.

1900 Target Large Frame: 1921-1941

Using the large frame Model 1900 this .22 rimfire double action revolver came with a 6 or 10 inch octagon barrel, oversize saw-handle shape checkered grips, and a 7 or 9 shot pull pin cylinder. The introduction of this revolver was part of the Iver Johnson Company's shift away from self-defense firearms to sporting arms after the First World War.

Target Sealed 8 First Model: 1932-1941

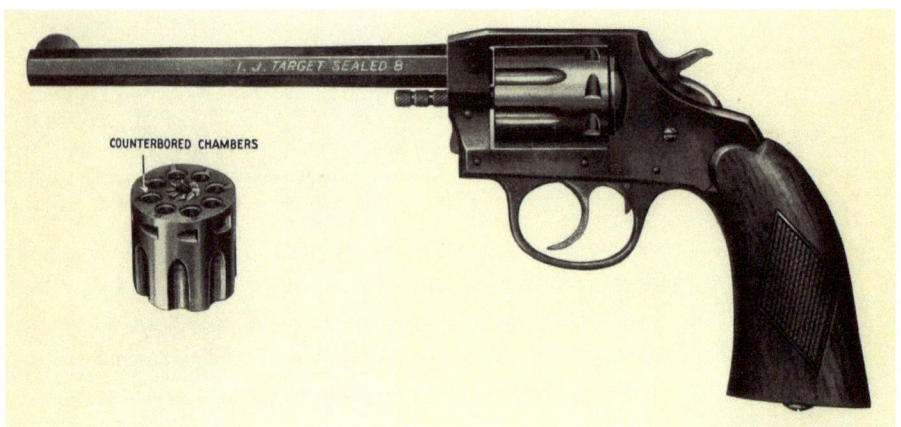

The Target Sealed 8 was an updated version of the 1900 Large Frame with recessed chambers that fully enclosed the cartridge case head. The Target Sealed 8 was available with an 8 shot cylinder, 6 or 10 inch octagon barrel and one piece checkered wood grips.

U.S. Revolver Company Model 1900: 1900 – 1946

U.S. Revolver Company small frame .22 caliber target pistol and a large frame .38 caliber.

U.S. Revolver Company was a brand name established by Iver Johnson for revolvers that were to be sold through the wholesale trade. The U.S. Revolver Company Model 1900 was a simply a low cost version of the Iver Johnson 1900. Instead of the octagon barrel and fluted cylinder of the Iver Johnson 1900, the U.S. Revolver 1900 had a round barrel and a non-fluted cylinder. The U.S. Revolver Company Model 1900 can be easily identified as it is marked "U.S.Revolver Co. Made in USA" on the top strap and U.S. on the hard rubber grips.

Lovell Safety Hammer Automatic (Eagle): 1887-1889

Sometimes referred to as the Model 1887, Model 1888 or Eagle, this double action, automatic ejecting .38 S&W caliber revolver was made by Iver Johnson for the J.P. Lovell Company. The Lovell Safety Hammer Automatic externally resembled the Lovell Swift of 1890-1894 and the Safety Automatic Revolver of 1894. However the frame was smaller than the Swift and it did not have the hammer the hammer action that would become famous on the Safety Automatic Revolver. The Eagle came only in nickel finish with rubber grips that have a dog's head design. The revolver is marked "Iver Johnson & Co. Worcester Mass. U.S.A. Pat'd April & July 20 1886. May 10 1887. Oct 16 1888." It is believed that the Model 1887 was only manufactured in 1888 and that production was under 5000.

Lovell Safety Hammerless Automatic: 1887-1889

Lovell Safety Hammerless Automatic.

A hammerless version of the Lovell Safety Hammer Automatic, this was the first revolver to have a manual safety on the trigger much like the modern Glock pistols of today. In order to fire the revolver the user must place a finger squarely on the front of the trigger. This revolutionary trigger safety was patented in 1886 and was used on all Iver Johnson Hammerless Revolvers until 1909. Made in .38 S&W caliber with a 5 shot cylinder and a 3 1/4 inch barrel, it was only available in nickel finish with hard rubber grip panels that had a dog's head design. It was marked "Iver Johnson & Co." on the top of the barrel.

Lovell Swift Hammer: 1890-1894

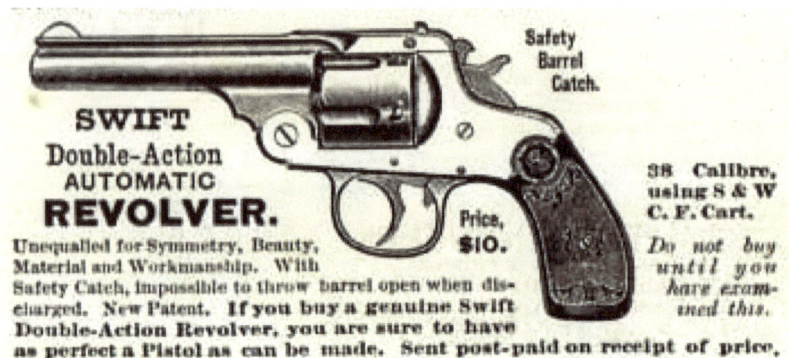

The Swift was made by Iver Johnson exclusively for John P Lovell Arms Company of Boston. A simple double action 5 shot .38 S&W caliber revolver, made with a nickel finish, the Swift revolver was the first Iver Johnson to use the owl's head logo on the grip panels. The owl's head grips would become a signature of future Iver Johnson products. Externally the Swift resembles the Safety Automatic Revolver that would be introduced in 1894 however there are several important differences. The latch for unlocking the frame pulls down rather than up. The ejector is slightly different. And most importantly the Swift did not have the hammer the hammer action that would become famous on the Safety Automatic Revolver. Due to the short production run the Swift is a relatively rare model Iver Johnson.

Lovell Swift Hammer with engraved frame and pearl grips.

Lovell Swift Hammerless: 1890-1894

A hammerless version of the Lovell Swift was also available. However it would seem it was not as popular as the hammer revolver. As a result it is quite rare. Specifications are the same as the Lovell Swift Hammer with the addition of a manual safety on the trigger, this manual safety insured that the user had to place a finger squarely on the trigger in order to fire the revolver.

Safety Automatic Hammer First Model: 1894-1896

Safety Automatic Hammer First Model.

A revolutionary design in 1894, the Safety Automatic Hammer was the first revolver to use safety as a marketing tool. Despite the name the revolver has no manual safety, nor is it an automatic. What made the Safety Automatic Hammer revolutionary was the fact that it had an internal transfer bar safety. This safety consisted of a separate hammer, transfer bar and firing pin. The hammer itself was not large enough to reach the firing pin. When the hammer was down the transfer bar would drop away. Only by raising the hammer would the transfer bar move into position allowing the gun to be fired.

Early revolvers made before the invention of the transfer bar were prone to accidental discharge if dropped with the hammer down on a loaded cylinder. In fact many owners would carry a revolver with one empty cylinder under the hammer for increased safety. This is a practice you can still see to this day in Cowboy Action shooting sports. Apart from its revolutionary safety features the Safety Automatic Hammer is an unremarkable double-action top-break, automatic ejecting revolver that takes most of its design from the Smith & Wesson break top revolvers of the 1860-70 period.

Available in a small frame 7 shot .22 rimfire, 5 shot .32 S&W, or a large frame 5 shot .38 S&W, both nickel and blue finish were available. Grips were the familiar owl's head design, however on both the First Model and Second Model revolvers the owl is looking towards the barrel. This was the first revolver marked "Iver Johnson's Arms & Cycle Works", however some early models were marked "Iver Johnson & Co.". You can identify the first model by its single top post barrel latch with a release lever mounted on left side of top strap and a cylinder that will spin when at rest. While production was short-lived some 250,000 were made from 1894-96.

Safety Automatic Hammer Second Model: 1896-1908

Safety Hammer Second Model in .38 Smith and Wesson (left) and .32 Smith and Wesson (right)

The Second Model was improved with a new double post top latch in place of the single latch of the First Model. The double top latch was easier to open as the user could simply pull up on the back end of the top strap. You can spot both first and second model revolvers as both have cylinders that will spin when at rest. Grips were the owl's head design with the Owl looking towards the barrel. Available frame sizes, calibers and barrel lengths were the same as the First Model. Some 950,000 Second Model guns were produced. Patent dates can be found on the top strap or left side of the barrel. "PAT'D APR, 6.86. FEB 15,87. MAY 10,87. MAR 13,88. AUG 25,96. PAT'D PENDING".

In 1901 anarchist Leon Czolgosz used a Second Model Safety Automatic Hammer to shoot President William McKinley.

Safety Automatic Hammer Third Model: 1909-1941

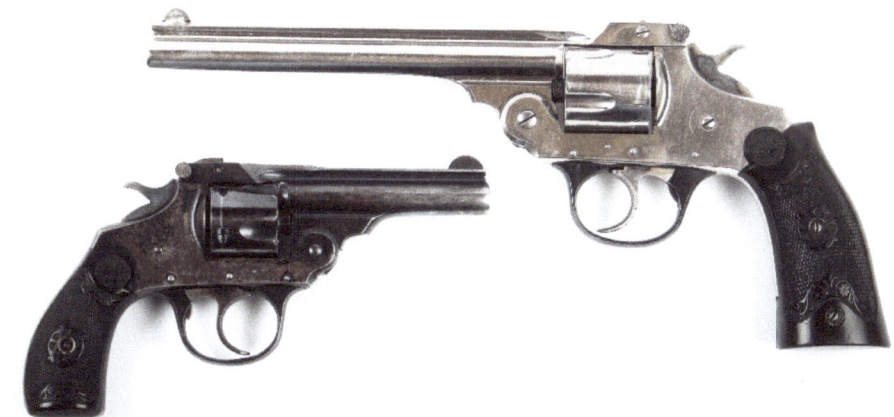

Safety Hammer Automatic Third Model in .32 Smith and Wesson (Left) .38 Smith and Wesson (right)

The Third Model looked much the same as the Second Model however it now had a coil spring rather than the flat spring of the first two models. More importantly it was now made to withstand the pressures of smokeless powder. You can quickly spot Third Model revolvers as they have cylinders that will not spin when at rest. Grips were the owl's head design with the owl looking down. However late Third Model guns are often found with wooden grips. Available frame sizes, calibers and barrel lengths are the same as the First and Second model.

The Double Post Top Latch used on Second and Third Model Guns.

Safety Automatic Hammerless First Model: 1895-1896

Safety Automatic Hammerless First Model in .32 Smith and Wesson.

This was a hammerless version of the Safety Automatic with a distinctive humpbacked shrouded frame and trigger mounted safety. This hammerless design allowed the pistol to be carried without risk of catching the hammer on clothing or other obstacles. However this feature prevented the revolver from being fired as a single action. The manual safety on the trigger was much like the modern Glock pistols of today. In order to fire the revolver the user had to place a finger squarely on the front of the trigger. You can identify the First Model by its single top post barrel latch with a release lever mounted on left side of top strap. Available frame sizes, calibers, barrel lengths and grips were the same as the first Safety Automatic Hammer model.

Single Post Latch used only on First Model Guns.

Safety Automatic Hammerless Second Model: 1897-1908

Safety Automatic Hammerless Second Model.

These Second Model Hammerless variants were updated with the double top latch in place of the single latch of the First Model. Second Model revolvers are identified easily by the double top latch and a cylinder that will spin when at rest. Available frame sizes, calibers and barrel lengths and grips were the same as the First Model.

Close up of the Glock Style Trigger Safety found on First and Second Model Guns.

Safety Automatic Hammerless Third Model: 1908-1941

Safety Automatic Hammerless Third Model in .38 Smith and Wesson (left) .32 Smith And Wesson (right).

The Safety Automatic Hammerless Third Model, also called the New Model no longer had the safety lever on the trigger. It was however updated with coil springs and was now made to withstand the pressures of smokeless powder. Owl Head grips can be found on early production revolvers with wood grips on late production. However the owl is now looking downward towards the base of the grip. You can spot Third Model guns quickly as the cylinder will not spin when at rest. Available frame sizes, calibers and barrel lengths were the same as the First and Second model.

22 Supershot: 1928-1931

The 22 Supershot was simply a dedicated target shooting model of the Safety Automatic Hammer. The Supershot was only available in a seven shot .22 calibre version with a six inch barrel. Marked "22 Supershot" on the barrel and having large wooden grips with a diamond pattern on the back the Supershot had a short production run.

22 Supershot Sealed Eight: 1931-1941 1945-1957

The 22 Supershot Sealed Eight was an improved 22 Supershot with a cylinder featuring recessed chambers that fully enclosed the cartridge case head. Recessed chambers make the firearm safer to use as they protect the user from flying debris resulting from ruptured case heads.

U.S. Revolver Co. Automatic Hammer: 1910-1935

U.S. Revolver Co was a brand name used by Iver Johnson's Arms & Cycle Works for revolvers to be sold through the wholesale trade. While resembling the Safety Automatic Hammer, U.S. Revolver Co guns did not have the famous Hammer the Hammer action and instead relied on a safety notch on the hammer. This simplification resulted in a lower cost revolver. The revolver was available in 2 frame sizes and 3 calibers, a small frame 22 rimfire with a 7 round cylinder and a 3 inch barrel, a small frame in .32 S&W calibre with a 5 round cylinder and 3 inch barrel, a large frame .38 S&W calibre with a 5 round cylinder capacity but a 3 ¼ inch barrel. Available in blue or nickel finish with hard rubber grip panels. Grips with "U. S." at the top were standard however large oversize two piece hard rubber grips were optional.

U.S. Revolver Co Automatic Hammerless: 1910-1935

This was a double action only hammerless version with a rebounding hammer. The Hammerless Model was only available in a small frame .32 S&W caliber, or a large frame .38 S&W caliber both with a 5 round cylinder capacity. Available finish, grips and barrel lengths were the same as the Hammer model.

Secret Service Special Hammer: 1912-circa 1923

Secret Service Special Hammer in .38 Smith and Wesson.

Iver Johnson made this revolver for the Fred Biffar Company of Chicago, one of the major supplier to Sears and Roebuck. Except for the markings on the barrel and grips the Secret Service Special is the same revolver as the U.S. Revolver Co. Automatic. The top of the barrel was marked "for .32 SMITH & WESSON cartridge" on the small frame revolver or "for .38 SMITH & WESSON cartridge" on the large frame. "SECRET SERVICE SPECIAL" was marked on the left side of the barrel and the grips were marked SSS. However special grips with imitation diamonds or American Flags could also be ordered. Unlike the U.S. Revolver Co Automatic, the Secret Service Special was not offered in .22 cal.

Despite the name the Secret Service Special had nothing to do with the United States Secret Service. The name was simply a marketing technique designed to capitalize on the reputation of the United States Secret Service. After the assassination of President William McKinley in 1901, Congress requested that the Secret Service provide presidential protection. This event naturally received a lot of press attention and made the Secret Service a household name.

Secret Service Special grip with American Flag insert.

It should be noted that Iver Johnson was just one of at least five companies that manufactured revolvers marked "Secret Service Special" for Fred Biffar Co. Other known manufactures of the Secret Service Special were Hopkins & Allen, Harrington & Richardson, Meriden Firearms Co and some of the later guns were made in Spain. Biffar used the name 'Secret Service Special' from sometime around 1902 until the late 1920s or early 1930s.

Secret Service Special Hammerless: 1912-circa 1923

The Secret Service Special Hammerless is the same revolver as the U.S. Revolver Company Automatic Hammerless except for the Secret Service Special markings on the grips and barrel. Unlike the U.S. Revolver Co Automatic Hammerless, the Secret Service Special was not offered in .22 cal.

Secret Service Special Hammer with Hammer Block Safety: 1917-circa 1923

Secret Service Special in .32 Smith and Wesson (left) and in .38 Smith and Wesson (right). Photos not to scale.

In 1917 the Secret Service Special was updated with a newly patented hammer block safety. This makes the Secret Service Special one of the few revolvers to ever be manufactured with a manual safety. The safety can be found located just above the grips. Grips are marked "SSS". The safety is stamped "PAT MAY 22 1917"

Close up view of the hammer block safety.

Secret Service Special Hammerless with Hammer Block Safety: 1917-circa 1923

Secret Service Special Hammerless Revolvers in nickel and blue finish.

The hammerless version of the Secret Service Special was also updated with the new patented hammer block safety.

Credits

Images
13,14,15,16,17,19,23,24,25,26,27,28,31,32,34,37,39,46,47,49,50 51,52,53,55.57,59 courtesy of Rock Island Auction Company.
http://www.rockislandauction.com

Images 29,30,40,42,43,44,45,48 courtesy of Rick Bryan Photography.

All other images author's collection.

Genealogy research courtesy of Olive Tree Genealogy.

Special thanks to Lorine Massey and Ernest Reid.

www.ingramcontent.com/pod-product-compliance
Lightning Source LLC
Chambersburg PA
CBHW041307110426
42743CB00037B/25